SOCKS

THE RULE BOOK

An Hachette UK Company
www.hachette.co.uk

First published in Great Britain
in 2016 by Mitchell Beazley,
a division of Octopus Publishing Group Ltd
Carmelite House
50 Victoria Embankment
London EC4Y 0DZ
www.octopusbooks.co.uk
www.octopusbooksusa.com

Distributed in the US by
Hachette Book Group
1290 Avenue of the Americas
4th and 5th Floors
New York, NY 10020

Distributed in Canada by
Canadian Manda Group
664 Annette St.
Toronto, Ontario, Canada M6S 2C8

ISBN 978 1 78472 133 6

A CIP catalogue record for this book is available from the British Library.

Printed and bound in China

10 9 8 7 6 5 4 3 2 1

SOCKS

THE RULE BOOK

10 essential rules for the wearing and appreciation of men's hosiery

MITCHELL BEAZLEY

CONTENTS

INTRODUCTION

'SOCKS ARE A SERIOUS BUSINESS.'

We wear socks every day (please *see* **RULE No. 1**, the first and most important rule, which covers this very point), and hopefully we change them for a clean pair just as frequently. We spend endless hours trying to find them – well, one of a pair anyway. There are times when we have to say farewell, when we have to face up to the sad truth that the days of our favourite pair of socks are well and truly numbered. This sadness is quickly overcome by a dose of sock retail therapy, that exciting time when you purchase a new favourite pair, or even more likely pairs, of socks. Sock ownership is truly an emotional journey.

We also spend a great deal of time trying to figure out the correct approach to the many different aspects of socks, such as wearing occasions, material choice, and colour and pattern selection. Most of our sock knowledge comes from parents and well-meaning friends, and sometimes from less well-meaning strangers who wish to impart their own advice. Whether that advice is asked for or not does not seem to matter. In fact, sock rules have long been assumed, and are often misinterpreted. No one has gone on the record to spell out clearly and unequivocally what the rules of socks actually are. Not until now, that is.

This book clearly, though perhaps not always concisely, lays out the ten rules of socks. No longer will you live in fear of sock faux pas, or even sock faux pairs. Prepare and steady yourself; mastering the ten rules of socks will change your life, maybe even for the better.

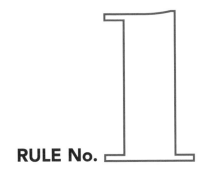

RULE No.

SOCKS MUST BE WORN

'SOCKS MUST BE WORN FOR ALL OCCASIONS
WHERE CLOTHING IS APPROPRIATE,
AND IN SOME INSTANCES EVEN
WHEN IT IS NOT.'

The non-wearing of socks, being *sans sock*, going sockless is inexcusable, not allowed, a red-card occasion. Anyone seen in this state should be shunned by polite society. This is the number-one rule for the very good reason that it should never ever be broken. If you accept and respect this rule, then the rest is plain sailing.

A BRIEF HISTORY OF SOCKS

Man first came to appreciate socks when he fashioned a pair out of animal skin, using a technique known as naalbinding (the binding together of materials with a needle – we could have just said 'needle-binding', but we were trying to be clever). The word sock comes from the old English 'socc', meaning 'light slipper', which, in turn, was derived from the Latin soccus, a lightweight, low-heeled shoe.

The oldest pair of socks to have been discovered was actually a split-toe design, which indicates they could be worn with sandals. Yes, you read that correctly – socks and sandals (*see* **RULE No. 7**). So, before we go off at a tangent, and more than likely a ten-page rant, let's just leave that one there and move swiftly on.

In the 8th century BC the Ancient Greeks decided that making socks from matted animal hair would be a wise move to provide warmth. Then the Romans, being singular of mind, as well as partial to a straight road or two, decided that they would wrap their feet in leather. You could argue that this actually sounds more like a shoe, but who are we to disagree with the might of the Roman Empire?

By AD 1000, socks were so revered that they were a way for the nobles of the time to show off their wealth. It appears that this trend is still very much in evidence today, the only difference being that you don't have to be a member of the royal family to show people your sock game (*see* **RULE No. 10**).

In 1589 an English gentleman by the name of William Lee, residing in Nottingham, invented the stocking frame knitting machine, specifically for the manufacture of stockings (think long socks, rather than other less pure thoughts). This industrial revolution – we stole that term from somewhere – enabled socks to be produced six times faster than by hand knitting, making socks more affordable and attainable virtually overnight. Individuals, and also a few premium hosiery companies, still produce hand-knitted socks in small quantities. This truly artisan skill demands great craftsmanship, which is evident in the retail price of hand-knitted socks.

The first machine-knitted socks were made from wool, since the machine could handle coarse fabrics only. From 1598, after improvements had been made to the machine (the version 2.0 of its day), other finer materials, even silk, could be used for machine-knitted socks.

The real breakthrough occurred, however, when the demand for a cheaper sock made from a less expensive material resulted in cotton socks being produced in abundance. The machine-knitted cotton sock industry has gone from strength to strength, from its humble beginnings in the 17th century to what it is now, a vast global business.

THE ANATOMY
OF THE SOCK

The **CUFF** is the opening at the top of the sock. Cuffs are usually formed with a rib stitch, so that the sock clings to the leg and doesn't fall down. The cuff is a very important part of the sock, as you don't want to risk exposing naked leg flesh. *See* **RULE No. 4**.

The **LEG** of the sock is knitted as a tube. For the majority of socks, such as ankle socks, this tube is straight. For longer socks, ones that sit above the calf, it is usually shaped so that the sock will fit the wider part of the leg, resulting in a game of two calves.

The **HEEL** is usually constructed in two parts, the **HEEL FLAP** and the **HEEL TURN**. The heel flap provides reinforcement over the Achilles tendon, the area where shoes tend to rub against the sock. The heel turn cups the ball of the foot.

The **FOOT** of the sock covers the top of the wearer's actual foot, and tends to be constructed in the exact same way as the leg of the sock. In a patterned sock, the pattern will more than likely continue down the leg to this area.

Very much like the human soul, the **SOLE** is the immortal essence of the sock. It is also the underside of the foot area. In ribbed and most patterned socks, this area is kept plain, so that it is smoother and offers superior comfort.

The **TOE** is where the sock in tube form is finished. Starting at the base of the wearer's toes, it narrows towards the tips. Toe seams, where the tube and the toe of the sock are joined, that are placed higher up on the sock tend to offer more comfort. A hand-linked toe is superior in finish and comfort factor than a machine-linked toe, which will give a noticeable ridge at the seam.

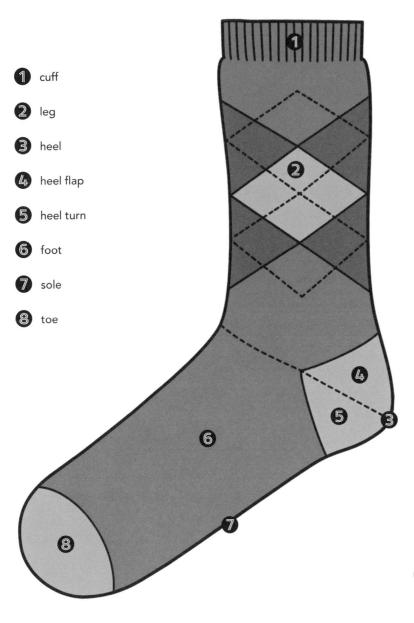

1 cuff

2 leg

3 heel

4 heel flap

5 heel turn

6 foot

7 sole

8 toe

HOW SOCKS ARE MADE

Industrialization and automated-knitting processes have outdated Grandma and her rocking chair as the go-to operation for getting socks made – sorry, Grandma. Modern sock-producing factories engage a vast array of expensive manufacturing equipment to look after the various processes that go into making socks.

RAW MATERIALS

Once the raw materials – cotton, wools, synthetics and blends for example – for a specific sock type have been chosen, they are washed, spun into yarn and most likely dyed to the required colour. Factories tend to buy finished yarn from external suppliers and store it in large yarn spools until needed.

KNITTING

These days, this is an automated process. The design, generated via a computer software programme, is digitally uploaded to a specific computerized circular knitting machine. Yarns are fed into the machine and a vast number of needles combine them in a series of interlocking loops that form the chosen style and pattern.

SEWING

At first, the sock looks like a tube. The finished tube is turned inside out and, in a process known as linking, the toe part is joined to the body of the sock. Mostly, this is done by automated linking machines, to increase efficiency and reduce cost.

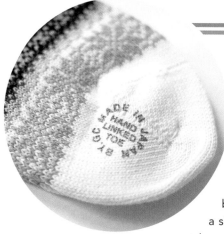

HAND-LINKED VERSUS MACHINE-LINKED TOES

Premium sock manufacturers still hand-link their socks to provide superior comfort and quality. Some specialist machines can actually replicate this, and the end product is called hand-linked. However, for supreme quality, the hand-linking process is best done by an actual living, breathing human being. It's a skilled task, the most skilled in the factory, and takes many years to learn. The loops on the two sides of the toe seam are linked with thread, one by one, using needles arranged in a circular set-up. The hand-linking process creates a much less bulky, more comfortable, flat seam than machine linking. The true sock aficionado will be able to tell the difference between a machine-linked and hand-linked toe with ease, and will only ever wear hand-linked socks.

WASHED AND DRIED

After the sock has been constructed it is usually washed and dried. This process is undertaken to shrink (so that future shrinking will be minimal) and stabilize the sock.

BOARDING

The socks will then be placed on a sock-shaped stretch frame. In the past these frames were made of wood, but metal frames have superseded them. The socks are steam pressed between two heated surfaces, to help give the sock its proper shape and appearance.

PACKAGING

Slips of card are attached at the opening, cuff or, to use its proper name, welt of the sock. (You know the ones – they provide all the company's details, material, construction, wise words and what have you, and you spend a good five minutes trying to find a pair of scissors small enough to use to cut the thread holding the card and your two socks together, without cutting the socks themselves.) The socks are then boxed and, in their fine splendour, are ready to be shipped.

IMPORTANCE OF SOCKS AND INVESTING IN QUALITY

Purchasing a reputable brand of socks is obviously fundamental. Knowing the lineage of your socks, knowing that love and care has been put into each and every pair, provides confidence that you have made the correct and wise choice in your purchase. Quality socks, albeit costing more, are more comfortable and tend to last longer. Finding a sock brand that you like and respect is just one decision on your journey to sock nirvana, or even sock pearl jam.

FIBRES

We make choices on a daily basis, from deciding what to spread on our toast in the morning and which mode of transport to take to work, to whether to tell the boss that we have to go due to family commitments when in reality we just want to knock off early for the day so that we can take part in a bit of sock retail therapy. And this is where one of the most important choices comes into play – which fabric or fabrics should you choose?

BAMBOO

Yes, bamboo. We're guessing you probably didn't expect that one as our first fabric of choice, but bamboo has a place in this list of hosiery materials. When cared for properly, bamboo is a very soft and breathable fabric, with the added advantages of being naturally odour repellent and antibacterial. Bamboo also has thermal regulating properties, thus helping to keep your feet warm in the colder seasons and cool in the warmer seasons. It's newer to the game than most of the other fabrics on this list, but you shouldn't overlook having a pair of bamboo socks, or two, in your rotation.

COTTON

Cotton is a remarkable, natural fibre, soft and smooth to the touch. It retains its shape, even after continuous wear and washing, keeps its colour well and has abrasion-resistant properties. Cotton soaks up water, several times its own weight, and is stronger wet than dry. Different types of cotton are used in the manufacture of socks.

COTTON LISLE This is given one more twist per inch (2.5cm) than ordinary yarns in one direction, with a second thread twisted at the same rate in the opposite direction. These two strands are then twisted together to create one combined thread.

Cotton lisle is a mercerized cotton. The mercerizing technique was invented way back in 1844 by John Mercer. (We have no idea where he got the name for his technique.) The yarn is exposed to a caustic-soda solution, which heightens the cotton's natural properties, and removes any rough fibres, leaving the yarn smooth, with a beautiful sheen finish and extra strength. As well as being a shinier and stronger yarn, cotton lisle is more comfortable on the skin, and gives a more durable end product than other cotton fabrics.

PIMA COTTON Pima cotton is a variety of strong-fibered cotton, developed from extra-long staple Egyptian cotton that was grown in America. It gets its name from Pima County, Arizona, where it was developed on an experimental farm, which sounds far more sinister than it is (we can neither confirm nor deny reports that the US government wanted to rename this Area 52).

If you see socks labelled as using Pima cotton, this is a very good sign of a quality cotton fabric and most definitely not a sign that government forces are wanting to infiltrate your sock drawer.

19

MEDIUM-LONG STAPLE AND EXTRA-LONG STAPLE COTTONS Staple is a commonly used term to describe average length of fibres. The longer the staple the easier it is to spin, so with longer staples you can get a much finer and higher-end product. Shorter staples produce a hairier sock. Look out for a note on the packaging saying that longer staple cotton has been used.

SILK

How do you fancy wearing a pair of socks made from a natural fibre that has been produced by insect larvae to build a cocoon? Good, then silk is for you and the mulberry silkworm is your go-to guy. Silk is smooth and has a very soft texture, much softer than synthetic fibres. It is expensive, due to the fact that it has to be harvested and cannot be man-made, but think of the aforementioned benefits. So a wise ploy, if you want superior finish and feel to your socks, may be to invest in your own silk farm.

BLENDS AND SYNTHETICS

NYLON

The invention of nylon in 1938 revolutionized sock manufacturing. Strong and hard-wearing, it is used as a coating for natural fabrics, such as cotton or wool, and when woven in this way, adds strength, stretch and durability.

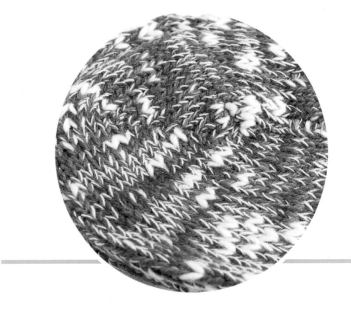

LYCRA

Lycra is the brand name for a synthetic that is used for its strength and stretchiness. It can be stretched to several times its initial size and then go back to its original shape and form. Considering the number of times you pull your socks on and off, there's a great deal to be said for them including Lycra, or some other durable and stretchable fibres.

WOOLS

Wool is a fantastic natural fibre, available from well-meaning sheep and other fine flocks. It has good heat retention, and the fibres also have some moisture-wicking capability, which can be vastly improved when blended with synthetics. Wool socks are a comfortable choice for colder days, but once you have decided upon them, some further choices have to be made.

MERINO WOOL

This is, more often than not, the wool of choice for high-grade sock brands and manufacturers. Merino is actually the name of the breed of sheep from which the wool comes. Merino sheep are famed for having arguably the

finest and softest wool of the sheep family. So when on your sock retail tour, be sure to ask your superior sock salesman for merino wool, to ensure the highest quality.

CASHMERE

We have the British to thank for cashmere. Well, we have the British to thank for changing the original word Kashmir to cashmere, the yarn having been manufactured in Nepal, Mongolia and, of course, the Kashmir region of south Asia, for over a thousand years. Contrary to popular belief, cashmere is actually a hair, not a wool, sourced from the hairy coat of goats. The coat's fine underdown must be separated from the thick, coarser layer before being converted into yarn – a laborious process, making cashmere expensive to produce.

Cashmere is fine, light and very soft, much softer than regular wool fibres. This makes it incredibly comfortable to wear but also less durable than other fabrics. Durability is dependent upon the percentage of cashmere used – the higher the percentage of cashmere, the less durable the material will be. Cashmere is great for bed socks, but when it comes to wearing cashmere socks all day, our recommendation is not to have these in heavy rotation and to save them for special days, to help prolong the life of your socks.

VICUNA

The vicuna is a relative of the llama – we are led to believe that they are still on speaking terms. It lives in South America and, to its continued pride, is the national animal of Peru. Vicunas are thought to be ancestors of the alpaca, with whom they are, unfortunately, not on speaking terms – something to do with bragging rights over wool softness.

Vicunas produce very small amounts of extremely fine, and extremely expensive, wool – finer and more expensive than cashmere. They can be shorn just once every three years and, since they roam wild, first they have to be caught.

The yarn doesn't take too well to the chemical processes in dyeing, so vicuna socks are mainly found in their natural caramel colour. In the past, it was law that only Incan royalty could wear vicuna. However, thankfully, sanity has prevailed, and anyone who has upwards of £500 or $1000 to spend on a pair of vicuna socks can safely do so. That's a relief, then.

CASHMERE/POLYESTER
MADE IN KOREA

RULE No.

CARE FOR YOUR SOCKS

'SOCKS SHOULD BE CARED FOR, TREASURED AND TREATED WITH THE RESPECT THEY DESERVE.'

Whether you are running, walking or even sitting, you are applying downward pressure on your feet. When you walk, each time your heel lifts off the ground it forces the toes to carry one half of your total body weight. In one day this force can equate to hundreds of tons. When running, the pressure on your feet is even greater and can be as much as four times your body weight (there is, of course, an easy solution to this problem – don't run). When you put your socks on or take them off, you are pulling and stretching them each time. Wear and tear is a natural occurrence. It is true that a premium pair will tend to last longer, due to the use of higher-grade materials and superior craftsmanship in the construction. The truth is, though, your favourite pair of socks will wear out and have to be replaced. The rules that follow will not halt the inevitable, but they will help prolong the life span of your socks.

STORAGE

SOCK DRAWERS – AN INSIDER'S VIEW

If the sock was invented on day one, then surely on day two came the sock drawer. This simple device neatly and cleverly holds and protects your sock collection. If you are a true aficionado of the sock game, you will probably have a set of sock drawers. If you are just starting out and earning your sock stripes, a single drawer will suffice.

Many devices are available to add compartments to your sock drawer for further ease of storage and separation. But whether you choose to follow this route or not, the main question here is in what order to store your socks, order being the appropriate word. Without order there would be chaos, and no one wants sock chaos (sock chaos theory – why can you only ever find one of a pair?). We go with a colour option and sort socks by their main colour (plain or patterned), dark to light – black, navy, dark colours through to light colours, ending in white. This will help you to find that perfect pair of socks to go with your outfit choice. Patterned and printed socks often offer a conundrum. The Rule of Sock here is to go with whichever the main colour is, and sort appropriately.

SOCK ROTATION

This is covered in full in RULE No. **8**, but it is pertinent to mention here that, as well as by colour, your socks should be arranged by season of wear. In summer, it is not appropriate to have your thick wool socks holding prominence in your sock drawer. Likewise, in winter, you should not have your invisibles on display (we are aware that comment is something of an oxymoron). Organize a back-up storage solution – separate drawer, canvas bag or similar – and rotate your selection, thus making it easier both to manage and find your sock selection for the season in question.

FOLD, DON'T ROLL

When sorting and managing freshly laundered socks, the vast majority of people will adopt the grab, turn and roll technique, thereby submitting their socks to unwanted and unnecessary stress and leaving them desolate in a ball of sock fury. I mean, how would you feel if someone grabbed you, turned you inside out and left your innards on show? Exactly!

Never ever do this to your socks. Instead, you should lay your socks together flat, one on top of the other in perfect symmetry. Then, to ensure

that they remain in perfect harmony, and together, in your sock drawer, you should fold over the top of the socks only, at the cuff. This clever technique will ensure that you are not unduly stretching the fabric and the socks will retain their shape and also have a better chance of a longer life.

WEARING AND WASHING

Let's be very clear about this. Human beings sweat – granted, some more than others, but all of us do it. The parts of your body you encase more than others will certainly sweat at some point because you are not allowing your skin to breathe. High-quality sock choice, and also appropriate shoe

selection, helps to deal with this issue, but will not prevent it. So you need to change your socks once a day. We have heard some people profess that with something like a wool sock you can go for longer. No, you need to change your socks once a day, as an absolute minimum.

We would even go so far as to suggest that if you are venturing out in the evening, you should change your socks. Nothing beats being able to walk tall with the appropriate amount of swagger (confidence, not arrogance) in a fresh, crisp pair of newly laundered socks. Your friends will appreciate it; small children and dogs, who are closer to ground level, will appreciate it even more.

HAND VERSUS MACHINE WASHING

Water, some kind of soap or detergent, and abrasion or rubbing things together – the combination of these three is how items of clothing are cleaned. (We include socks in this category, and cannot abide it when retailers insist on putting socks under the, wait for it, 'Accessories' section of their websites. Socks are clothes, too. Have you no shame, retailers?) Changes in how these three areas are delivered can result in amazing life prolonging or shortening

effects. Water too hot, detergent too harsh, abrasion too … er … abrasive – all these variables can, and do, contribute to doing more harm than good to your socks.

This is why we always recommend that you hand wash your socks. Cotton-based socks may stand up to regular machine washing better than most other natural fabrics, but you still run the risk of the socks losing their colour, or their soft fabric being too roughly handled by your industrial washing machine. If you insist on a machine wash, we recommend as cool a temperature as possible, using a non-biological detergent. Do not subject your socks to a spin cycle and do not put them in the tumble dryer – hang them to dry instead. To ensure that your socks remain in pairs, we suggest using plastic sock clips to keep them together while they are being tortured in the washing machine – after all, misery loves company.

Hand washing is the best way to preserve your socks. Wools, specifically cashmere, must be hand washed. The best way to hand wash your socks is to use warm, not hot, water, a non-perfumed soap and a gentle rubbing action on the areas that get the most wear, such as the heels and the toes. In fact, this is such a serious matter, something that really needs to be done properly, that we're spelling it out in a step-by-step approach:

1 Fill your sink, bucket or Jacuzzi with warm water (not hot, but not cold either, because cold water won't kill the bacteria that live in the dirt).

2 Add soap – mild liquid soap is best – and mix it into the water.

3 Add socks.

4 Completely submerge your socks in the water and allow them to soak for about thirty minutes.

5 Knead by hand, ensuring all areas are covered but paying specific attention to the toe, underfoot and heel of each sock.

6 Gently squeeze the water out of the socks and place them to one side.

7 Empty the dirty water from the sink, bucket or Jacuzzi.

8 Fill the sink, bucket or Jacuzzi with warm water – no soap, just warm water.

9 Put your socks back into the water and let them soak again for up to thirty minutes.

10 Remove the socks, gently squeeze out excess water and hang them up to dry.

There you have it, the easy and somewhat time-consuming ten steps of sock hand washing. So after that's all done, Sunday is over and it's probably time to go to bed with the smug satisfaction of knowing that you have the best looked after and cleanest socks in the land. Your friends, family and work colleagues will be so envious when you tell them how you spent your entire Sunday.

IRONING SOCKS

So once you have spent all Sunday hand washing your socks, now comes the question of how best to care for them before placing them back in the sanctuary of the sock drawer. Ironing your socks – yes, no, maybe? The answer is an emphatic YES.

While heat is not your friend when it comes to washing your socks, it can be your ally when used carefully to iron creases and wrinkles out of them. We do recommend ironing all your socks. Again, care is important. Ensure that the socks are just slightly damp, not wet, before proceeding. If they have dried completely, lightly spray them with water on both sides. Place them flat on the ironing board and make sure you iron them evenly, with a smooth motion, on both sides.

And there you have it, an almost completely new-looking pair of socks. Only thirty-seven more pairs to go and that's your Monday off work finished with, you lucky person, you.

MENDING

Darn it, sometimes the inevitable happens. No matter how much care and attention you lavish on your socks, a dreaded hole appears, usually in the toe area. (Prevention tip – cut your toenails more frequently!) Often your favourite pair is affected – you know, the ones that go best with the sneakers you currently have in rotation, or your favourite shirt. If you can't find an exact replacement, or a suitable alternative from your sock drawer, it's time to get darning. Here are ten surefire steps to darning a sock:

1   Get a light bulb.

2   Yes, really get a light bulb; or, if you want to be fancy, a darning egg.

3   Turn your sock inside out and place it over the light bulb.

4   Thread a needle, but do not tie the end because this will give a bulky repair and leave you with an unwanted raised seam.

5   Start sewing a running stitch approximately ¾in (2cm) above and on either side of the hole.

6   Continue this, moving closer to the hole.

7   When you hit the hole, keep going with the running stitch across the hole.

8   Keep going until you reach the other end of the hole and finish approximately ¾in (2cm) away from the hole. Cut the thread.

9   Now repeat this process but at right angles and weave these stitches under and over the current threads. Finish when you have covered the hole completely.

10 Put the light bulb back in the lamp.

That's how to rescue your sock from the sock graveyard – so much easier than buying a new pair.

LOST ART

Leaving aside the character played by Jeff Goldblum in *Jurassic Park*, there are actually very clever people out there who study chaos theory, the science of the unexpected. Chaos theory explores the area where things are impossible to predict or control, such as how Jeff Goldblum got the role of a scientist in *Jurassic Park*.

Chaos theory has its most natural application in the world of socks. You can use all the preventative methods at your disposal, but you will never be able to stop one of a pair of socks going missing. This is going to happen – scientific fact. It's possibly the most frustrating thing that can ever happen to you. You've got the outfit dialled, shoe game on point, shirt that matches the pants, and all you need is that one pair of socks to complete your look. But you can only find one of the pair. It doesn't matter how many butterflies flap their wings in China, you'll probably never find that other sock again, and the harsh reality is that you have to learn to deal with it and move on.

Next time you get dressed, start with the socks and work the outfit around them. With that starting point safely secured, predictability will once again triumph over chaos, and you will be at peace with the universe.

SAYING GOODBYE

Inevitably, the time comes to consider whether to keep or to let go. This is the hardest of times. You have studiously looked after your socks. Hand washed them, ironed them, darned them and kept them immaculately on the appropriate rotation in your sock drawer, wrapped individually in tissue paper (this may be a step too far, even for us), but to no avail.

You put them on for the last time. You look down and see your skin peeking through at the heel, you notice that the fabric is not as smooth as it once was and is obviously pilling, and you observe that they are beginning to sag at the cuff opening, no matter how many times you pull them up. This is the time of realization – these socks need to go.

It was the best of times, when all your friends complimented you on your sock game. It was the worst of times, when you could only find the left one (thankfully, you were reunited with the right one later, when you found it in the bottom of the laundry basket). But now it's time to say goodbye. The worst mistake you can make is thinking that you can get a couple more wears out of them. You'll know, your friends will know, and even strangers will know, that your sock game is not where it should be. It's time to go shopping for a new pair.

RULE No.

USE OF SOCKS TO BLEND IN OR TO STAND OUT

'SOCKS SHOULD BE APPROPRIATE TO YOUR OUTFIT AND ALSO TO THE OCCASION.'

Originally, when there was not much choice of colours, styles, fabrics and patterns (we call this the Sock Dark Age) the rule of thumb, or toe, was for a gentleman to wear socks one shade darker than his suit – mid-blue suit, navy sock, for example; light grey suit, dark grey sock. With the advent of greater choice and a more casual approach to dressing, this rule is now outdated. These days, matching your socks with your chosen outfit is slightly more complex.

SUITING

A gentleman, no matter whether his work dictates the need for it or not, should own a minimum of one good suit, and if just one, a sombre one is a pertinent choice. His suit will then be suitable for a job interview, a wedding, a funeral, a first introduction to the prospective in-laws or attending a fancy-dress party as one of the Reservoir Dogs.

A simple and easy option would be to choose a suit in a plain fabric in black, navy blue or grey. If you're feeling brave, adding more texture and interest by choosing a fabric such as a gabardine or one with a subtle herringbone pattern (subtle as in tonal to the base fabric) can lift the suit. Braver still – but don't push it – would be a check pattern a couple of shades darker than the base cloth, or a thin pinstripe, but that should really only be on a navy blue base. Don't go so far as a chalk stripe unless you are re-enacting a scene from *The Great Gatsby*.

The choice of socks to go with your suit should match the occasion and make you and those around you feel comfortable (a sign of both a true gentleman and someone with a strong sock game). It's easy to fall into the trap of using socks and accessories (tie, pocket square or miniature poodle) to show your inner rebel and flamboyant, rakish but confident style. However, for formal events it is better to employ a more subdued approach. This will enhance your appearance and provide a more confident look. Play safe and choose the darker shade of socks to match your suit – you can always add a tonal pattern if you wish.

At a slightly less formal event, but where a suit is still required, it is perfectly acceptable to stray to a lighter colour option, say a light blue sock with a dark navy suit. The rule here is that if you are going to be more daring with your socks, choose a tie (if you are proposing to wear one) to match them as closely as possible. If going for very bright and vibrant colours, stick to a plain sock option. You should have one stand-out element only, either colour or pattern but not both together.

For anything remotely resembling a formal occasion, the above is as far as you should push it. We would recommend staying away from contrasting colour patterns and multi-coloured sock options. Save these for a much more casual occasion. When wearing dress shoes with a suit, you should only ever wear dress socks. These are finer and more lightweight than everyday socks, made of cotton lisle or merino wool, for example. Heavier weight, bulkier socks tend to ruin the line of the suit pant at the hem and, in addition, the sight of socks spilling out over the top of a leather dress shoe is not an attractive one.

TOWN AND COUNTRY

In these modern times, the suit is no longer the go-to outfit at many work places, although not as rare as the bowler hat or the umbrella. (We hear that there is definitely a call for a comeback on the latter; not the former, though, unfortunately.) However, a gentleman must still look professional, although more relaxed, in his working wardrobe. A smart shirt and trousers, teamed with a pair of leather-based shoes, is the norm.

CITY DWELLER

Obviously, time of year and climate are factors here (see **RULE No. 8**) but a fairly relaxed dress code at work offers an opportunity to be more daring in your sock choice. You still want to come across as the consummate professional you are, so stay away from novelty or themed socks in the work place. Socks with images of recreational plants, despite their undoubtedly relaxing effect, would not necessarily help you win that promotion and corner office you have been hankering after. Outside of this, bright colours that match an item in your overall outfit, or patterns – whether they be checks, argyles or stripes – where

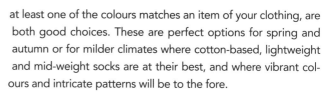

at least one of the colours matches an item of your clothing, are both good choices. These are perfect options for spring and autumn or for milder climates where cotton-based, lightweight and mid-weight socks are at their best, and where vibrant colours and intricate patterns will be to the fore.

Striped socks are always a fail-safe option for office wear. They are smart yet casual. For a more formal look, go for a thin stripe with only two colours. A three or more coloured stripe gives an added casual element, and you can even push it to a thicker stripe but not as thick as a block stripe. This is not recommended for office wear because it can look as if you have forgotten to take off your football or rugby socks.

We do go back to the rule that there really should be just one element that draws significant attention. If you have decided that summer time in the office means that the Thomas Magnum, P.I. (surely the only man who can pull off a moustache with the desired effect) Hawaiian print shirt gets an airing, best to downplay your sock choice in regard to patterns. Bright colours, ideally ones that match the body colour of the shirt, would work best. If opting for a plain shirt, you can go much wilder on your sock pattern choice – by all means bring those killer floral print numbers into play.

In the colder months, you could neatly avoid the Christmas jumper and adopt the style of a gloomy yet strangely charismatic Scandinavian detective by wearing a snowflake-patterned or Fair Isle knitted wool sweater. Be sure to accompany it with some heavyweight wool socks and casual winter footwear. Best to stay away from knitted patterns, though, and broadcast your Scandinavian allegiance with a two or three-coloured thick yarn. If you are still sporting a more formal shoe, go for a mid-weight, finer-gauge option, applying the same rules as before.

The work place can be a minefield when trying to ascertain the correct dress code. Let the office environment and formality be your guides to your sock choice. You should never be afraid to push the boundaries, but be sure to make choices that enhance your confidence rather than cause you to worry about their effect on others. The socks with the subliminal print depicting an image of your favourite NBA basketball player that went down so well with your mates last Saturday night may not be appreciated in quite the same way by the CEO on Monday morning. Wearing a freshly laundered

pair of fine-gauge, herringbone-patterned socks that colour match your outfit to perfection may just give off the air of confidence and authority that will land you that parking spot and bonus come year's end.

PARK AND OUTDOOR LIFE

Even the urbanites among us feel the occasional need to escape the concrete jungle and venture outdoors, be it a trip to the local park or the nearest mountain range (which will involve travelling abroad if you happen to live in Holland). All these outings, whether long or short, should be tackled with the appropriate choice of sock.

Camouflage socks, obviously, are perfect for the outdoor environment (*see* **RULE No. 5**). Choose your type of camouflage pattern wisely, dependent upon the natural vegetation. Southeast Asian tiger stripes actually work better on socks in a northern hemisphere urban environment than they do outdoors. This may sound strange, but try it and you will see that we are right. Woodland camouflage works very well, and if travelling to more barren areas, desert camouflage is the clear choice.

Outdoor life calls for a more rugged and tougher look than the thinly striped or delicately patterned socks that are best left to towns, cities

and pavements. Go with a mid- to heavyweight option (temperature depending). Argyle is a great pattern that actually transcends this boundary and arguably works better in a rural setting. Wider stripes work well, as do Fair Isle and other patterned options.

DENIM

When Levi Strauss asked Jacob Davis to help construct a pair of work pants to meet the needs of the American blue-collar worker, the denim jean was born. It is a riveting story, and one that we strongly suggest you investigate. The denim jean has changed somewhat since that time some 150 plus years ago, but the five-pocket denim pant has become a symbol of Americana and is worn worldwide.

Dark denim is generally the preserve of the modern gentleman, and a fairly narrow leg and leg opening are currently the fashion. (Some stalwarts out there refuse to bend to modern trends, and are still resolutely wearing a looser, boxier classic jean, reminiscent of the 1950s styling and fit. To those plucky few, we salute you!) Denim works just as well with formal shoes as it does with more casual styles and trainers, giving myriad wearing opportunities and great potential.

Navy socks with dark blue denim? If it's plain navy, the answer is absolutely not. They blend in far too much and end up looking like weird extensions of the leg. But navy in combination with one or more other colours or with patterns? Absolutely yes. The body colour of the navy sock will work as a great background and that means you can be as bold as you like with the other colours or patterns. Similarly, a different coloured sock with navy or dark blue contrast colours or patterns will lift the whole look in a way that will complement the denim.

Black socks, plain or patterned, should be worn with denim only if the rest of the outfit is black. If the shoes and top are black, this is a strong look. If the shoes or top are of another colour, you run the risk of looking like you are wearing your school uniform socks on the weekend – black is too much of a dark and stark contrast unless paired with itself.

Lighter coloured socks and denim are a peril best avoided. Better denim fabric will be naturally indigo dyed and in a raw state, thereby introducing you to the world of denim bleed. Indigo dyes do not penetrate the

yarn, meaning that they tend to rest on top of it. This results in the dye chipping off from the top of the yarn with wash, wear and abrasion, and when you wear light-coloured socks, the dye will quite happily find a new home there, giving your expensive pair of socks a new denim hue.

TRAINING SHOES

Whatever name you have for them – trainers, plimsolls, pumps, runners, or even sneakers if you must – these shoes were once the preserve of athletes and vindictive physical education teachers. They never left the playing field. Now they are a ubiquitous part of our everyday wardrobe, and it is crucial that your sock choice is on a par with, and as considered as, your choice of trainers.

Around the world, most people initially got socks and trainers incredibly wrong, wearing plain grey, black or even beige socks (who, but who, in their right mind would wear a beige sock?). The Americans, however, got it right, teaming their Converse Chuck Taylor High Tops with long

white tube socks. When pulled up to the knee, as they liked to wear them, this combination made the legs of already tall basketball stars look even further accentuated. While in some parts of America folk have resolutely stuck with the white sock (*see* **RULE No. 6**), the more modern and forward-thinking urban cities of the US of A, along with the rest of the world, have moved on.

With the exception of white trainers, with which you must wear a contrast sock option outside of the gymnasium (once again, *see* **RULE No. 6**), you can go tonal on all colours – black with black, navy with navy, pink with pink – neatly ensuring that the blending-in part of the rule is observed.

It gets trickier with multi-coloured and patterned trainer choices. The correct approach is that the more detail, colour and pattern on the training shoes, the more subdued the choice of sock should be. This doesn't mean that you can't wear a multi-coloured sock, or that you have to stay away from patterns. What you must do, if you are wearing a 'statement' training shoe, is ensure that your sock choice complements your shoe choice and does not detract from it.

RULE No. 3

RULE No.

SOCK COVERAGE, HOW MUCH TO EXPOSE OR HIDE

'SOCKS SHOULD COMPLEMENT AND COMPLETE YOUR OUTFIT AND LOOK. THEIR USE SHOULD BE IN PERFECT SYNERGY AND ENHANCE YOUR BEING.'

Not only do socks come in various fabrics, sizes, colours and patterns, but they also come in different lengths. And, of course, there are rules for socially acceptable sock length, dependent on outfit choice and wearing occasion.

The first and most important rule is that when wearing trousers, no leg flesh should ever be exposed and on display when standing, seated or even lying down. On all these occasions, no skin should be visible between the bottom hem of the trouser and the sock; your socks should completely cover this area at all times. There are few things more unsightly in this world than a gentleman exposing naked lower-leg flesh.

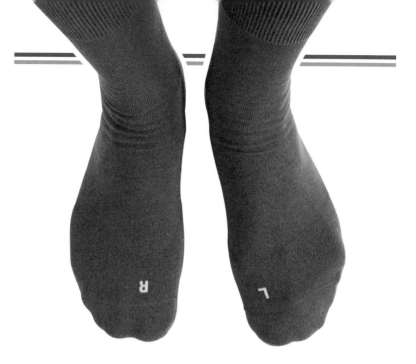

SOCK SIZING

One size does not fit all. Just like a bespoke suit, your socks should fit you like a glove – or at least like very well-fitting socks. Too tight and they'll cut off your circulation and not allow your feet to breathe. Too loose and you run the risk of them wrinkling around your ankles, exposing skin, and also bunching inside your footwear, resulting in a less than compelling look as well as discomfort.

The ideal start is to look for asymmetrical socks that offer a left and right option, a simple invention and production method that was first patented in America as far back as 1887. We are led to believe that the original construction meant that the end product was not the most comfortable, but a revised process was invented by Franz-Josef Kalde, who was employed by the Falke hosiery, leading to small, medium, large and extra large size runs.

Better still are sock brands that offer more intricate and varied sizing options that correspond with your shoe size. These are available from superior retailers, so if you can, do go there first. You'll find that you have socks that fit you as well as a bespoke suit from Saville Row, at a fraction of the cost.

TYPES OF SOCK

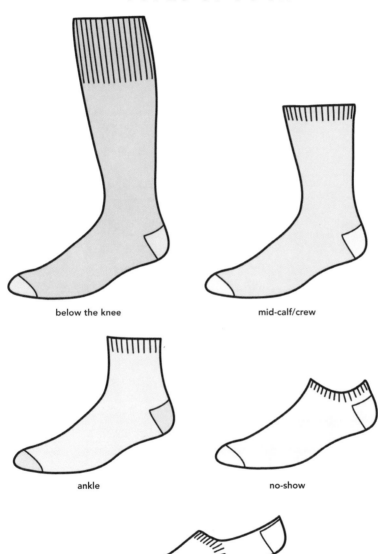

below the knee

mid-calf/crew

ankle

no-show

invisible

SOCK LENGTHS

BELOW THE KNEE

The Italians take sock coverage to a high level, quite literally. They have such concerns over this issue that their socks are made to be worn pulled up to just below the knee – extending above the calf but never over the knee (that would be a stocking, and that's a whole different book and set of images altogether). Below-the-knee socks are less popular in other countries, but these socks are a fail-safe option that guard against naked flesh exposure. Provided attention is paid to fabric and weight options that are appropriate to the season in question, they are also perfectly suitable to be worn all year round.

MID-CALF/CREW

Mid-calf or, as they are often known, crew socks are ones where the top of the sock extends above the ankle but not above the largest part of the calf. When worn correctly (pull your socks up!) and sensibly, socks of this length cover the important areas – a great all-rounder of a sock that looks good with any outfit.

ANKLE

An ankle sock, sometimes known as a quarter sock, covers the ankle area but does not extend more than one third up the calf. These socks should

only ever be worn with shorts for sporting activities. You may believe that you have made an acceptable decision by teaming them with a pair of trousers, but a simple test will show the error of your ways. Sit down. Have you exposed yourself? The answer will be yes. Now cross your legs. Have you exposed yourself even further? Again, the answer will be yes. So no, this is not an acceptable look.

NO-SHOW

As names for sock lengths go, the no-show is a bit of an oxymoron. These socks are designed not to extend above the opening of the shoe. However, a telltale small sliver of fabric can usually be seen at the ankle area. This is not a misdemeanor, nor a violation. It can actually be helpful since a fellow sock aficionado is easily able to tell that the wearer has not broken the first rule, thus saving embarrassment and the issuing of an on-the-spot fine. No-shows are only ever to be worn with shorts and never with trousers.

INVISIBLE

As its name suggests, the invisible sock is never seen in public – just like a politician's innate ability to lie, you know it exists but it is very difficult to prove. The invisible wraps the foot at the base, from toe to ankle, but does not extend up to the opening of the shoe. It is to be worn with caution and with sympathetic and comfortable footwear only, as this sock does not offer any protection in the heel area. Once again, this sock length is only ever to be worn with shorts. There is a trend for wearing this type of sock and its cousin, the no-show, in warmer months, with leather dress shoes and trousers. Many a man can be spotted daring an on-the-spot fine by showing their ankles. This behaviour is not to be condoned, and we can only hope that the perpetrators of these travesties quickly see the error of their ways, stop flaunting their ankles, and go out and buy some decent, proper length socks.

TROUSER LENGTHS AND HEMS

The issue of exposure does not relate to flesh alone. It also covers the question of how much sock it is permissible to show at any one time. Obviously, if you have spent a large sum of money on some vicuna or cashmere numbers, it would be selfish not to let people see them so that they can appreciate your sartorial excellence for themselves. However, it is not always pertinent to flaunt too much sock.

FORMAL TROUSERS

A standard rule to follow is that the more formal the situation or event, the less sock should be on display. If you are attending a funeral, it is not the done thing openly to display your socks. Instead, wear trousers that hit the top of your footwear when you are standing. The same goes for a black-tie event, when a tuxedo is required. With a tuxedo, you should only ever wear black dress socks, and no matter their fine quality, exposure should be kept to a minimum.

A related question is whether to cuff or not to cuff your trousers (turn ups being another term). A cuffed trouser is one where the extra fabric at the bottom has been turned up and is held in place by stitches at the side seams. Cuffs can serve to accentuate height and also protect trousers from fraying and other damage at the seam of the hem. Edward VII is recognized as the originator of cuffed trousers, in the 1890s. In most European countries, cuffs for formal suit trousers are not the norm these days. Although not a bad option, they are not generally recommended. The Americans, on the other hand, have been firm fans of the cuffed formal trouser since the early 20th century, and continue to be so.

If you do wish to have a cuff on a pair of suit trousers, we would recommend that the leg opening is on the narrow side. This will give a much better line and look. Height rule for a cuff is 1in (2.5cm) for a gentleman who stands up to 5ft 10in (1.78m), and 1¾in (4.5cm) if taller.

A good, tailor-made pair of trousers without cuffs will be cut on a slant, with the front of the trouser covering shoelaces when the gentleman is standing. This is a good look, clean and smart, that will show just a hint of sock when standing or walking, and slightly more sock – but, importantly, no flesh – when seated.

CASUAL TROUSERS

Cuffs on casual trousers, corduroys, chinos, and other cotton-twill based options are much more common across all continents. They are perfectly acceptable and are actually better suited to a more relaxed-fit trouser that is wider in both the top and lower leg. When resting on the shoe, the cuff should be flat and cover both shoe opening and shoelaces. This somewhat reduces the opportunity to showcase your socks, but it can be a classic, clean look.

A more modern trend is to go with a casual trouser that sits above the shoe, on the ankle. This provides a modicum of space between shoe and trouser for the wearer to display his sock of choice, daring or otherwise. We highly approve of this trend, with two caveats – it is best suited to narrow-leg trousers that taper from knee to hem; and no cuffed hems, because these add unsightly bulk at the ankle and detract from the clean lines and slimming properties of a good pair of narrow-leg, tapered trousers.

Lastly, in the area of casual trousers, we come to elastic, an ingenious invention by Thomas Hancock, the fine gentleman who also brought us vulcanization and other wizardry with rubber. When worn with cotton-twill trousers, elastic waistbands are the preserve of the style ignorant. Elasticated hems are allowed, however – there is a modern trend for jogger pants, a hybrid of a chino and a sweatpant with a trouser-style top, complete with fly, waistband and belt loops. (Here's a trouser rule for free: if you're wearing trousers with belt loops, you must wear a belt.) These have the advantage of adjustable length. With the aid of an elasticated hem, which will stay neatly in place, you can show more or less sock, as you choose. We would suggest that jogger pants are to be worn only with trainers and never with leather shoes.

RULE No. 4

DENIM JEANS

Once you've tackled the formal, casual, cuffed, non-cuffed dilemmas, you could be misled into believing that you know all that there is to know in the trouser department. Well, you are almost there, but not quite. No section on sock exposure would be complete without discussing height options with the denim jean. Here we detail the five options, which you can either ignore or use to abuse the hems of your jeans.

NO CUFF

Most likely, you'll be buying your denim off the peg. If you're very lucky, you will find a pair that nestles neatly on the top of your shoes, but if you like a clean, no-cuffed hem, you will probably need to have the jeans altered so that the hem fits just right. If taking this approach, ensure that the thread the tailor uses matches the colour of the original thread. Ideally, the tailor will use a chain stitch, so that you get that distinctive roping effect reminiscent of jeans of old. However, before having your new jeans altered, make sure you know whether they have been sanforized, pre-shrunk or are shrink-to-fit. You do not want to go through the time and expense of having them altered only to find out that they are now gently caressing your ankle bone rather than your shoes.

SINGLE CUFF

This is a simple manoeuvre to deploy when the jeans may be just a touch too long. Simply turn up your hem from inside to outside just once, exposing the 'wrong side' of the fabric and the inside of the seam on the hem. The recommended height is to turn up just 1in (2.5cm). You can, of course, experiment with different heights, but we recommend keeping it clean and simple.

DOUBLE CUFF

Follow the same steps as for the single-cuff option, but do one more turn. This time you will expose just the inner workings of the jeans, not the inside of the hem, creating what is arguably a cleaner cuff/turn-up option than the single cuff. Do, however, bear in mind that the thickness of this cuff can have a less than desirable effect on your perceived height. This is the most common modern version of cuffed jeans, because it suits most individuals and looks.

EXTRA-WIDE SINGLE CUFF (BUCKET)

The extra-wide single cuff, or bucket cuff, was first employed by American cowboys and blue-collar workers who had no time, opportunity or money to have their jeans altered. It is relevant today if your jeans are excessively long, you do not want to have them altered and you are brave and particu-

larly tall. Shorter gentlemen should stay away from this option, because it makes the legs look shorter. Follow the steps for the single cuff above, but keep going, keep going, keep going still, then stop. The bucket cuff works best if you really go for it – aim for a height of 4in (10cm) or more.

This look is best worn with a sturdy pair of boots (think classic Red Wing Moc Toe); otherwise the cuff can dwarf your footwear and make your feet look ridiculously small. Also, it is best carried off with a jean jacket, for that double-denim look, and an 'I've just built a railroad single-handedly across the plains of America' middle-distance stare.

PIN ROLL

The pin roll, also called the tight-rolled or pegged cuff, is the origami of denim hem rolling and to be attempted only by a true master. The pin roll rose to fame in the late 1980s and early 1990s, when the youth of the time wanted to showcase their footwear and sock game.

To achieve a champion-level pin roll, put on your jeans and follow these steps:

1 First, do a single cuff; this gives the hem additional rigidity to stand up to the task ahead.

2 Take up the fabric at the hem and pull the front of the leg away from you.

3 Fold the extra material, the part not encasing your ankle, back on itself and turn it over and up.

4 Follow step three once more for heavyweight fabrics (14oz denim or more) and twice for mid to lightweight fabrics (less than 14oz).

5 Take the excess material and fold it inward into itself to form a neat nip and tuck.

The less skilled may use safety pins to keep the cuff in place – this just means that you need more practice. It is also common and acceptable, especially on heavyweight denim, to re-do the pin roll during the day. The look can be worn with slim, regular or loose-fitting jeans or casual trousers. The pin roll adds a taper to the leg, and when done well and falling at the correct level (at the ankle), it can add perceived height to the wearer. Not only will the pin roll show off your footwear and sock game, it will also stop the denim bleed from jeans ruining your shoes. Do be careful with overly loose trousers, though – they have a habit of wrinkling down, covering the pin roll and giving a less than desirable look.

RULE No.

PLAIN, PATTERNED AND PRINTED SOCK WEARING

'PLAIN, PATTERNED AND PRINTED; ALL THREE
ARE ACCEPTABLE DEPENDING UPON WEARING
OCCASIONS AND OUTFIT CHOICE.
THE DECISION, THOUGH, MUST ALWAYS BE
A CONSIDERED ONE.'

Sock selection across the realms of plain, patterned or printed can be confusing, what with all the choices on offer. However, with full consideration and the right application, this is the area that offers most opportunities for fun and self-expression. Here we break down the main focus points to help with your choices. Firstly, don't mix stripes and checks in your outfit, because that will end as badly for you in the outfit stakes as crossing the streams does in *Ghostbusters*.

PLAIN: PRIMARY COLOURS

RED

Red can add that additional kick to an outfit if you're feeling courageous, outlandish or just want to draw attention to who you are and what you're about. Red says danger and can therefore be seen as aggressive, so it is best teamed with more subtle footwear that will calm your outward appearance.

BLUE

Blue, in its various shades from light through to dark navy, is the stalwart colour of the male sock drawer. Blue socks are to be sought, bought and kept in numbers, because it is tough to find an outfit that blue won't either complement or complete. It can be dramatic when dark, calming when light and a good leveller in mid shades. There is a good reason why boys are dressed in blue. Your mother wasn't wrong, so respect her wishes and keep wearing this colour to the full.

YELLOW

Yellow usually comes a distant second to red in the 'going all out' look, and is a subtle contrast colour. It is best when paired with navy and denim, and adds a great fresh hit of colour to an outfit.

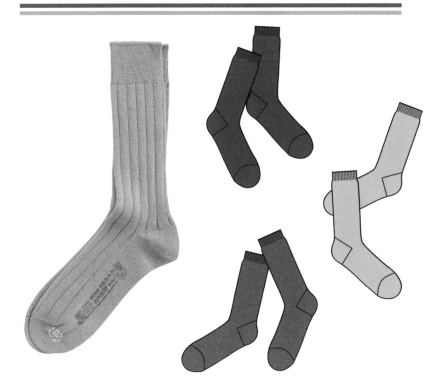

PLAIN:
SECONDARY COLOURS

ORANGE

We're biased, but we simply cannot get enough of the colour orange in our sock selection. Plain bright orange socks give the fresh hit of a red or yellow pair, but without the suggested danger or subtlety. This colour works just as well with navy and denim outfits, looks outstanding with black and can even lift a grey look. The colour orange, we salute you.

PURPLE

We believe that there is a place for purple in the sock drawer. It works best on formal occasions, either with a grey suit (a darker shade of purple) or a navy suit (lighter and brighter shades of purple). Worn with black, it can make the wearer look as if he is off to the blood bank, so unless that is where you are going, this combination is best avoided.

GREEN

We like greens when venturing outdoors – they work best in their natural habitat, among like-minded shades, and look fantastic as a casual option with denim and brown leather trainers or shoes. Greens tend to work less well in a more formal environment, or as dress socks, because they do not mix well with the usual suiting options of navy or grey. We're also not fans of green socks and black suiting; this combination just doesn't sit well with us. Our advice is to finish your greens in a casual environment and stop making such a fuss.

PLAIN:
NOT A COLOUR

BLACK

Plain black socks are the only choice for a very formal occasion. Black is a sobering and sombre colour and gives a formal outfit the desired level of courtesy and professionalism. Black socks can also be worn casually, paired with a black T-shirt, shirt or jacket; in this way, they level out the outfit.

WHITE

see **RULE No. 6**

PLAIN:
OTHER COLOURS

PINK

It takes a real man to wear pink. If you have a fair complexion, we would suggest staying away from pink socks, because they will drain colour away even further. For everyone else, we say go for it.

BEIGE OR TAN

Beige for a pair of trousers or a jacket, yes; for a pair of socks, no. We cannot think of any outfit that is accentuated, lifted or improved by the addition of beige socks. They are usually seen worn with sandals (*see* **RULE No. 7**) and shorts by geography teachers; if that is not enough to dissuade you from having a single pair in your sock drawer, we don't know what is.

RIBBED SOCKS

Made up of vertical ridges – the more technical term is 'wales' – of different widths, ribbing is arguably the most common pattern in both dress and mid-weight plain-coloured socks. Not just a design element, ribbing has a practical application by giving socks much-needed elasticity, without having to resort to the use of synthetic fibres for added stretch. Ribbed socks are a good classic staple when you want a simple plain sock in your life. Often the design is lifted with a bright contrasting coloured toe, heel and cuff.

STRIPES

Knights of old displayed their allegiances, in combat or in tournaments, with striped cloths in various colours. This heraldic use of striped cloth survives to this day. Medals signifying civil and military honours hang from striped ribbons, the colour, width and placement of stripes depending on the specific decoration. Stripes are the go-to pattern for sock aficionados as they lead the heraldic struggle and daily combat that is the sock game. Striped socks are a must-have in the sock drawer and in your sock rotation.

   The general rule of sock here is that the narrower the stripe the more formal the look, and, conversely, the wider the stripe the more casual the look. If you are wearing more than one stripe in your outfit, they must be of different widths. Most striped socks are found in the horizontal form, but vertically striped socks are also available and these have the added advantage of appearing to lengthen the body.

BENGAL STRIPE

Bengal stripes are solid vertical stripes that are usually approximately ¼in (6mm) wide. A vertical stripe can lend an outfit drama and boldness, and our recommendation is that if you are going to go for this look, really go for it and pick a sock that involves multiple colours.

PENCIL STRIPE

Pencil stripes, also known as dress stripes, are thinner than candy stripes but wider than pinstripes. The width between the stripes varies from cloth to cloth, and the stripes tend to be uneven. The pencil stripe is the go-to stripe for every occasion – more formal with two alternating colours, more casual when three or more colours are used.

PINSTRIPE

The narrowest members of the stripe family, pinstripes are more common on shirts and suits, where they tend to signify a very formal and classic cloth. They can be found in sock form, though, and are best worn in the same formal way. Pinstriped socks complete an outfit best when just two alternating colours are used.

CANDY STRIPE

Another member of the vertical stripe family, candy stripes tend to be wider than pencil stripes but thinner than Bengal stripes, usually about ⅛in (3mm) wide. The name comes from the stripe pattern found on sticks of rock, a confectionery made famous by English seaside resorts that have never been famous for their marvellous weather. When in sock form, our recommendation for the candy stripe is to push the boundaries of the colour spectrum and go for more than the standard two-tone design.

RUGBY STRIPE

This stripe gets its name from the socks that form part of a rugby player's kit. (Rugby was invented when a plucky young gentleman, playing football at Rugby School, thought he would be better off picking up the aforementioned ball and running with it.) Generally, these socks, have thick horizontal stripes. At home or away, on lightweight or heavier weight socks, they are best worn in a semi-formal or casual manner.

CHEVRON STRIPE

Chevron stripes are made up of diagonal stripes that go up and down in zigzags, offering an alternative to a classic horizontal stripe. They look great on dress socks and add a modern take to a formal outfit. Best not worn with either a striped or checked suit, as the clash can be too much for the eye.

CHECKS

GINGHAM

The gingham pattern, or basketweave as it is also known, is formed by horizontal and vertical stripes of the same colour that cross each other on a white background, forming even-sized checks. Gingham originally started out as a striped pattern and was woven into a check pattern during the middle of the 18th century. Blue and white and red and white combinations are generally the most popular. This pattern looks great in sock form when worn semi-formally with a freshly laundered shirt and a pair of jeans. Never to be worn to a picnic or barn dance, for obvious reasons.

TARTAN

Tartan consists of vertical, horizontal or diagonal interlocking stripes of different colours that criss-cross to form different sized checks. Tartan is not exclusive to Scotland, nor is it the preserve of natives of that country, and it can be a great way to add colour and depth to your sock game. It's best to stay clear of mixing tartan socks with suits and other formal attire, however, since they are casual in nature. The only additional rule to mention here is that if anyone offers to sell you tartan paint, politely decline the offer.

HOUNDSTOOTH

The popular houndstooth pattern is formed of small checks that look broken, uneven and pointy, not unlike a hound's tooth. Traditionally, this is a black and white pattern, but a variety of colours are now on offer. It looks great on fine dress socks, which accentuate the detail involved, and is at its best when teamed with a suit for a formal look.

HERRINGBONE

Although it is not officially a check, we didn't want to exclude this classic pattern, with its distinctive rows of inverted v-shapes reminiscent of a fish skeleton. It is regularly used for suiting and overcoats as well as socks. For that man-about-country look, perfect for shopping in town for a new Land Rover, team herringbone socks with a smart pair of dark denim jeans and a tweed jacket, in herringbone of course.

MINI CHECK

Mini check looks close to a gingham but the checks are a lot smaller. It is a more casual pattern than, say, a narrow stripe, but more formal than larger check patterns. Wear it with a casual outfit for a weekend jaunt in either town or country.

WINDOWPANE CHECK

This pattern is made up of very wide checks, usually in white on one main body colour, that look like windowpanes. Due to the subtlety of colour usage, you can wear this sock with a plain or checked suit for a formal look.

SPOTS OR POLKA DOTS

Polka dots are a generic term for pretty much any pattern consisting of a base colour with either single or multi-coloured dots in contrasting colours. The word polka comes from Poland and literally means 'Polish lady'. It's the name of a dance from that part of the world, and this pattern first found fame at the time the Polka became popular. In modern times, a pattern of filled-in circles is fine for the male of the species, and offers a nice alternative to a stripe or check. Polka-dot socks also make a good contrast to a striped or checked shirt, and these can and should be worn together for this very effect. Go with small dots for formal occasions, extending to larger versions for a more casual look.

FAIR ISLE

This pattern is named after an island in northern Scotland. Fair Isle is a traditional knitting technique used to create patterns with multiple colours. Socks in the Fair Isle pattern look best when made with heavyweight wools, cottons and cashmeres, and worn with a sturdy pair of leather brogues or other such footwear. This pattern is definitely for a casual look and suited to the colder months.

ODD SOCKS

The very thought of wearing mismatched socks is abhorrent. This idea can only have been born out of laziness or – even worse – bad sock management. At some point, an individual who could not even be bothered to search for a matching pair thought that he could brazen it out in polite society with a devil-may-care attitude and different coloured socks. It is likely that the wearing of odd socks will draw attention, but highly unlikely that it will be welcome attention. It looks like it says – odd. **THE RULING IS CLEAR – NO.**

73

CAMOUFLAGE

The word camouflage comes from the French word camoufler, meaning to disguise. Camouflage patterns were used first to conceal battleships, then land transportation and finally people.

The most commonly seen camouflage pattern is the woodland colourway of the disruptive pattern material, or DPM for short, first used by the British Armed Forces. It incorporates the colours of temperate western Europe – black, dark brown, a mid-green and sand. Although no longer standard issue battle dress – it has been replaced by the multi-terrain pattern – woodland DPM remains a favoured pattern across socks as well as clothing. Introduced in the late 1980s, the desert DPM features similar shapes, but comes in shades of brown, khaki and a very light sand colour. Tiger stripe camouflage patterns are associated with southeast Asia.

Camouflage socks make a great addition to your sock drawer for casual occasions. Wear them with trainers and a relaxed outfit. There is even an underground movement that promotes the regular wearing of camouflage, whatever the location, on a Tuesday.

A complete head-to-toe camouflage look, right down to the socks, should be reserved for those who are either serving in the forces or are going hunting in the woods with an American Vice President.

ARGYLE

This diamond pattern is actually based on a Scottish tartan, cut on the bias. It is knitted using the intarsia technique, and the diagonal lines are sometimes embroidered on afterwards. Popular on the golf courses of Scotland in the 1920s, the Argyle pattern was introduced to America by the president of Brooks Brothers, John Clark Wood, who discovered this fabric while on holiday in Scotland in the 1940s.

The most famous hosiery exponent of the Argyle pattern is the Burlington brand, which was originally founded in the 1920s, in Burlington, North Carolina. In 1985, the Burlington clip – a metal stud attached to one sock only – was introduced, apparently to differentiate the brand from other, inferior Argyle sock producers. Argument still rages about whether the Burlington clip should be displayed on the inside or outside of the wearer's ankle. This book doesn't rule on this point (the same applies to the Stance sock brand's logo embroidery). We leave it up to the wearer.

In our not so humble opinion, every right-minded gentleman should have an Argyle pattern, or several, in their sock rotation. It is most definitely not confined to golf courses, and if worn correctly, works as well in town as in country.

NOVELTY SOCKS

The advent of the novelty sock is probably not up there with the invention of television, the first man on the moon or even the time when Harry met Sally, but it most definitely had an impact, albeit not the most positive one.

To clarify, when we are talking novelty, we are talking about outlandish, brash and downright tacky sock designs. You know the ones – they feature Batman, Homer Simpson, Disney characters and Muppets among many others. The people who signed the licensing deals are guilty of allowing these images to be scandalously abused. And don't get us started on the novelty sock's partner in crime, the novelty necktie.

The novelty sock plague had its heyday in the late 1980s and early 1990s. It spent much of the year dormant, biding its time until conditions were right for it to multiply, around Christmas time. At one time or another, we've all felt the sheer horror of tearing off the wrapping paper to see a

brightly coloured cartoon face staring back at us, emblazoned on a fabric high in polyester.

How you respond to the novelty sock gift could easily make or break a family relationship for decades to come. This is an absolute minefield, so rehearse your gift acceptance look and speech. Emphasize the words 'thank you' and then ensure that you banish that pair of socks to the bottom of your sock drawer as soon as is humanly possible, never to see the light of day again.

The absolute steadfast rule is that novelty socks should never be worn by anyone old enough to wear long trousers. And if you ever see a novelty tie and sock combination headed in your direction, turn and run.

PRINTED SOCKS

Printing on fabric that has a certain amount of give and stretch has become easier in recent years, and delivers good results, so you can get pretty much what you want printed on a sock, whether your interests run towards hip-hop artists, recreational vegetation or the Mona Lisa's enigmatic smile.

The pattern is transferred onto a sock's surface under heat and pressure by a process called sublimation printing. Due to the rigours of this process, the socks used are made mainly of polyester, which may not be as comfortable as a cotton or wool-based sock, but what you give up in comfort you gain in the clarity of the print and vividness of colour.

The American nation has embraced this innovation and trend, and not just the large sock manufacturers, such as Stance. Such an accessible and affordable printing method has given birth to many a garage industry. Individuals take performance socks – the Nike Elite sock is a firm favourite – and print their own, or their customers', designs on them.

This version of the printed sock is not to be confused with the novelty sock. These are much more of a premium product and absolutely allowed. The only recommendation we give here is that if you are going to do it, then really go all out. Wear these socks pulled up high with shorts, or with a high-water level (we're talking flood-level) pin roll or turn-up on your trousers (*see* **RULE No. 4**). If you are confident enough to walk down the street with Eric B on one sock and Rakim on the other, then show the world that you know you got soul.

RULE No.

WHITE SOCKS

'WHITE SOCKS ARE A PERENNIAL MINEFIELD AND
BEST AVOIDED AT ALL COSTS.'

Are white socks ever permitted? The classic ruling on this has always been yes, but only on the sports field. This was fine when trainers were only ever worn when indulging in sporting activities. Times change, and so do rules. Now the rule is that white socks should never be worn with trousers. Yes, you heard us, never with trousers. Well, unless you're playing cricket, of course. When worn with long trousers by grown adults, white socks make the wearer appear adolescent at best. They do not convey the look of maturity or give the air of sophistication you desire. They may have seemed acceptable in your youth, when worn with a school uniform to indicate to your peers that you too were not afraid of a little rebellion and non-conformism, but they have no place in adult life when combined with a grown-up pair of trousers and outlook.

White socks with shorts and leather formal or semi-formal footwear are not allowed. White socks with shorts, whether they are designed for sporting activities or not, and trainers are allowed. A slight exception to this rule is that they are also acceptable if you are sporting the socks and slides look (*see* **RULE No. 7**) – arguably white is the only colour of sock that you should wear with this look.

The best and safest approach is to ban white from your sock selection completely. White clothes, whether a crisp new T-shirt, or a freshly laundered shirt, pressed and ready to go, have something compelling about them. If you dare to have white in your sock drawer, you may be tempted to flout the rule. Save yourself from embarrassment, and an immediate on-the-spot fine for rule breaking. Take yourself out of harm's way and eradicate white from your sock selection. Some rules are meant to be broken. This is not one of them

A GENTLE REMINDER
NO! NO! NO!

RULE No.

SOCKS AND SANDALS

'NO!'

Is the answer really that simple?

Remember the geography teacher who used your head as target practice for chalk throwing while sporting more synthetic fabrics than it should be humanly possible to wear at one time, thereby risking death by static shock? Socks and sandals were his foot attire of choice, keeping him firmly planted to ensure the perfect trajectory for his throw. His vast knowledge of glaciers and ox-bow lakes meant that, unfortunately, there was no room left in his brain for any ideas of sartorial elegance or the understanding of appropriate dress codes. So he teamed beige slacks with open-toed brown leather sandals, 'un-combined' with grey socks. Thanks to geography teachers worldwide, this look is completely unacceptable. However, there are other options that give rise to more positive answers.

SOCKS AND CLASSIC OPEN-TOED SANDALS

As per above, the response to this combination is abundantly clear
– AN ABSOLUTE NO.
THIS LOOK CAN NEVER BE TOLERATED.

SOCKS AND CLOSED-TOE SANDALS

We're talking Dutch-clog type footwear, and variations on this theme. The most popular modern versions come from German footwear manufacturer Birkenstock, in the form of Boston-style sandals. The Japanese have had a

positive influence on the trend for closed-toe sandal and sock wearing. The sock of choice is CHUP from Japanese hosiery manufacturers Glen Clyde, whose low-gauge woven socks are inspired by old Fair Isle designs.

The rule here is to make sure your sock is heavily patterned. If you're going to show this much sock, stand up and be counted – there is no point in keeping it plain. This is a look best completed with jeans or long trousers; and considering the width of the footwear, we would definitely suggest going with a wider hem on the leg. Do not attempt to carry off this look with a pin roll.

POOL SLIDES
(AN AMERICAN PHENOMENON)

Pool slides were once the preserve of European football stars, who wore them poolside in the off-season while reliving past glories and trying to forget tabloid sensations from the season past. They teamed their pool slides with rather embarrassing hairstyles (see the German national side from the 1980s) and very short shorts, but never with socks.

However, since then, Americans have embraced pool slides, wearing them for the most part with sports socks (white sports socks – *see* **RULE**

No. 6) for their own sartorial look. Doughboy, the character portrayed by Ice Cube in the 1991 film *Boyz n the Hood*, famously teamed his pool slides with shorts, a T-shirt and 40oz of liquor (we believe this part of the look to be entirely a personal choice and not a prerequisite). This look is most definitely to be worn only with shorts, mainly those of a sporting nature. With the socks pulled all the way up to below the knee, this is an acceptable look, but only in the summer months and with a liberal application of the right nonchalant attitude.

FLIP FLOPS

Flip flops to Americans and the British, thongs to Australians, are an acceptable form of footwear in some social circles, worn without socks. Obviously, if you choose to do so, you are contravening **RULE No. 1**, and by rights, we should stop right there. However, companies do exist that make socks specifically to be worn with flip flops, and you might expect us to embrace these. We do not. If you choose to wear flip flops that is an oversight. If you choose to wear them with socks, that is a slight – a complete taboo.

There is one variation to which we may turn a blind sock eye – the split-toed tabi sock from Japan, designed to be worn with traditional thonged footwear. Made for both men and women, these socks are acceptable only if worn with traditional Japanese dress, such as a kimono. The other concern here is that tabi socks are usually white. White socks! What a veritable minefield of contradictions and conundrums this sock game is.

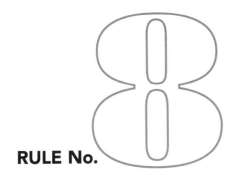

RULE No.

SOCKS FOR ALL SEASONS

'SOCKS ARE A SEASONAL AFFAIR, AND THE SELECTION SHOULD BE APPROPRIATE TO THE SEASON.'

The solution to making the right choice of seasonally appropriate sock lies, like other wardrobe choices, mainly in the fabric. Matching the season and climate with the correct corresponding textile is key. Thickness or weight of fabric is the deciding factor here, and most reputable sock manufacturers will inform you whether the sock you are considering is of the light, mid or heavyweight variety.

SPRING

Spring is when the versatile mid-weight sock comes to the fore. Whether cotton or wool-based, mid-weight fabric is the best choice for this season. This is the time of year when the full breadth of our sock selection comes into play, and just like newborn lambs frolicking in the pasture, you should push your sock game as hard as possible and earn the reputation as a true sock aficionado that you and your hard-spent bank balance have been focusing on for the past few months.

SUMMER

If you are lucky enough to live in a part of the world where you can expect a proper summer, you will need to deploy the lightweight options from your sock drawer. Whether these are crew socks, no-shows or invisibles, make

sure you remember the wearing rules discussed earlier in this book. Light-weight cotton and wool blends work best, but if the temperature increases, we would firmly recommend moving over to the cotton-based section.

AUTUMN

Autumn is the season of mists, mellow fruitfulness and a mid to heavier weight cotton or wool sock. We prefer a mid-weight wool sock for autumn. The weight, comfort factor and natural insulating properties of this fabric put it above cotton. A blend of wool and cashmere is possibly the most

appropriate, if slightly decadent, option. A cotton sock is obviously still a possibility, in which case you should go for a mid or even a heavyweight sock, depending upon the crispness of the morning.

WINTER

It's time to batten down the hatches. Heavyweight socks need to be moved to the front of the rotation right now. We would suggest going straight for wools and cashmere blends to help stave off the cold and reduce the risk of frostbite while you wait for the bus or train on your winter commute. Choose a tight, knitted, heavier weight sock for a more formal outfit – you don't want to go too bulky here. For casual attire, the thicker and warmer the sock, the better. Extra points are awarded for matching socks with a woollen hat or scarf, be it in colour or pattern. Minus points for a complete matching set of all three, because that smacks of auntie's Christmas present being taken out for a trial run.

CHRISTMAS SOCKS

Christmas may not truly be a season in its own right, but thanks to retailers, it tends to start earlier and last longer than winter itself. In any case, it would be remiss of us not to include it here, since the Christmas sock is fraught with danger. As discussed in **RULE No. 5**, in the area of novelty socks, the Christmas sock is rarely given an approval rating. Some Christmas socks – but let's be honest, more winter-themed, patterned socks – can and do make the grade. A subtle snowflake or a solitary reindeer with a traditional Fair Isle patterned backdrop can actually work, but brightening the colours, enhancing the patterns or adding trinkets count as definite rule violations.

When it comes to the Christmas-themed sock, invoke the three-point rule: one, never give; two, never receive; three, if two is out of the question, work on polite rejection. No one's sock drawer deserves to be tarnished with these monstrosities.

95

RULE No.

SOCKS, TRAVEL WITH CARE

'WHEN TRAVELLING WITH YOUR SOCKS, DUE CARE AND ATTENTION SHOULD BE PAID AT ALL TIMES.'

Within the safety of your home it is relatively easy to care for your socks – we're talking proper sock management here (*see* **RULE No. 2**). Issues may occur, however, upon leaving your residence, when you release your socks from their sock drawer and unleash them upon the outside world.

Selection is of paramount importance. The main factors to take into account are climate, occasion (whether formal or informal) and outfit pairing. Flexibility is also worth considering when making your final choice. Patterned socks containing colours that match all your clothing can make for a versatile and confident selection.

Once you have decided on your travel sock selection and the number of pairs you will be packing for a weekend away, a short trip or a long-haul adventure (given the proper care and attention, this can take longer than the actual journey itself), you must decide upon the best means to transport your socks.

SOCK CASE

For any trip longer than one week, the standard rule is always to travel with your sock case. Obviously, in this modern and civilized time, every household possesses at least one sock case. Our recommendation is a hard-shelled and lockable case, ideally with separate compartments, to ensure proper carriage. As soon as you arrive at your destination, hand your case over to the hotel staff to be taken to your room with the rest of your luggage. Strict instructions about how you, personally, like your socks to be unpacked and arranged (whether by material, colour or pattern) should be delivered at check-in. A good hotel will be used to such sock requests, and your demands will be greeted with a knowing nod and smile of fellow sock appreciation.

SOCK POUCH

For journeys of less than a week, short business trips or weekends away, you should transport your socks in a sock pouch. Most good gentlemen's outfitters and retail establishments will have a selection of canvas or leather bags that can be used for this purpose. The pouch with a zip closure is

recommended, but please use with care, as snagged socks are not a good look. A decent-sized pouch should hold three or four pairs of socks with ease. However, please note that the pouch should never be used for posing purposes. No one likes a show-off, and as you have already learnt, socks are a serious business.

SOCK LAUNDRY BAG

Here's the issue. You have safely transferred your socks from their designated sock drawer and their safe room (or perhaps your safe) at your house. However, you have packed insufficient socks for your entire stay (obviously, this contravenes RULE No. **2** and the laws of proper sock management, but we shall overlook this indiscretion for the time being). This means that you may well have to wash your sock selection by hand on your travels. We recommend this course of action, and suggest travelling with, or obtaining, a fragrance-free natural soap. A good hand scrub in the sink with soap and warm water should suffice (see the ten steps of sock washing in RULE No. **2**, a truly great rule).

The alternative, if you are under time constraints or incapacitated, is to leave your prized possessions to the mercy of the hotel laundry service. This should be your last resort, but if you must follow this route, we recommend using your own laundry bag. There is nothing worse than receiving a single lonely sock from an embarrassed hotel employee. A mid-weight cotton canvas bag is best, clearly labelled with your name on the outside. It is also a good idea to provide washing and care instructions inside the bag. You can never take too many precautions where your socks are concerned.

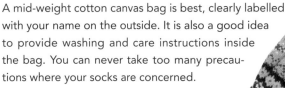

RULE No.

SOCK GAME

'SOCK GAME IS THE ART AND ABILITY OF
CONFIDENTLY AND COLLECTIVELY APPLYING
ALL THE NINE RULES OF SOCKS TO EACH
AND EVERY WEARING OCCASION.'

The tenth rule is a simple one to learn and subsequently follow: you must adhere to and apply all the previous nine rules.

In addition, you have to apply the rules in such a way that your sock choice is a considered one each and every time, appropriate to your outfit, appropriate to the occasion and, most of all, appropriate to you as a person. The socks and outfits you choose should tell people something about you. Whether it is as simple as complementing or enhancing the event you are attending or the mood you are in, your choice should be a positive reflection of yourself. If you're not into cycling, don't wear socks with images of bicycles on them. If you're at a formal occasion, printed socks are not the done thing. In a casual setting, you have the freedom to let your inner nature come to the surface, show self-expression and your personal sense of style.

Be confident with your sock decisions and your outfit choices. If you don't feel good the moment you put them on, change your socks for a better option. You need to be able to present your look to the world confidently. Above everything else, wear the socks, don't let them wear you.

OUR PARTING WORDS ARE PROBABLY THE MOST PROFOUND ONES IN THIS BOOK – HAVE FUN WITH YOUR SOCK GAME.

AFTER ALL, THEY ARE ONLY SOCKS. AND, JUST LIKE LIFE, SOCKS SHOULD BE FUN.

GLOSSARY OF TERMS

ABRASION The rubbing together of two separate bodies, in washing and wearing activities.

ARGYLE A diamond pattern; actually a tartan from Scotland cut on the bias.

BLENDS, FIBRES AND FABRICS Two or more different types of fibres mixed together to create a new fabric with unique properties.

CAMO TUESDAY An individual's right to wear camouflage patterns on a Tuesday.

CASHMERE A very soft hair fibre from Cashmere goats.

CLUB A place where like-minded individuals go to interact and discuss the most important and finer things in life, like socks.

COTTON A soft staple fibre that grows around the seeds of cotton plants.

COTTON LISLE Tightly woven cotton formed of two strands that have each been given an extra twist per inch (2.5cm) when compared to standard cotton yarns.

DRESS SOCKS Lightweight, fine-gauge socks, usually of a cotton or fine wool base, to be worn with a suit at formal occasions.

EMBROIDERY Entirely decorative stitching showing a pictorial design, or even wording, applied to a finished sock, thus providing embellishment and branding opportunities.

ERIC B AND RAKIM American hip-hop duo, famed for their use of samples and exceptional beats, lyrics and delivery.

HAND-LINKED TOE A superior process whereby the toe seam on a sock is closed by hand, giving an almost seamless and thus more comfortable toe.

IRONY, THE USE OF Not taking yourself too seriously.

IRONING Taking your sock management very seriously.

MACHINE-LINKED TOE An inferior process whereby the toe seam on a sock is closed by a machine, giving a noticeable ridge on the sock.

MEMBER 001 The unacceptable face of Sock Club London.

MEMBER 002 The acceptable face of Sock Club London.

MERCERIZED COTTON Cotton that has been through a treatment that strengthens it and also gives it a sheen.

MERINO WOOL Wool from the merino breed of sheep; tends to be finer and softer than wool from other breeds.

NOTED The appropriate response to a fellow sock aficionado's correct application of the sock rules.

ON-THE-SPOT FINE An immediate fine issued to someone who is in breach of the first rule.

OPEN-TOED SANDALS Footwear that is solely the preserve of geography teachers and other poor-style afflicted people.

PIMA COTTON Very soft and durable extra-long staple cotton.

PIN ROLL A high-rise cuff or turn-up on your trouser; turned and folded into place for maximum sock exposure.

SNEAKERS American name for trainers.

SOCK An item of clothing worn on the feet.

SOCK CASE A prefabricated structure used to transport your socks safely from place to place.

SOCK CLUB LONDON A collective of like-minded individuals.

SOCK GAME If you've got this far, we're guessing you've read the book. If you don't know what this is by now, we politely suggest you go back to page one and start again.

SOCK POUCH A small bag often made of canvas, always with a closure, used to transport a small number of socks safely.

SOCKS AND SANDALS No.

STAPLE Commonly used term to describe average length of fibres. The longer the staple, the easier it is to spin, delivering a higher-end product.

SYNTHETICS Man-made fibres that are created with enhanced properties compared with naturally occurring fibres.

RULES OF SOCK CLUB The ten abiding sock rules as clearly, but not concisely, laid out in this book.

TARTAN Pattern made up of crisscrossed horizontal and vertical bands in different colours.

TASTE Subjective.

THOMAS MAGNUM, P.I. A moustached legend; good taste in cars, bad taste in Englishmen.

THOMAS HANCOCK Inventor of elastic and the vulcanization process.

TOE IN SOCK The footwear version of the popular phrase 'Tongue in cheek'.

TRAINERS British name for sneakers.

WALES Term to describe the weaving of additional sets of fibres into a base fabric so that it forms vertical ridges. Also a country of the United Kingdom.

SOCK LIST

SOCK LIST

107

INDEX

Page references in *italics* are illustrations, those followed by 'g' are glossary entries.

ABOUT THE AUTHORS

Illustration: Josh Parkin

No apologies, No regrets

member 001 and member 002 are the founding members of Sock Club London, a members' club that sets out to promote and champion men's hosiery and associated style-related items. Sock Club London has a London home but a global reach, via its growing international membership base and Club events, as well as through its Blog and Instagram account. Sock Club London provides its members, who are allowed a certain anonymity by being known only by their membership number, with regular updates and information on men's style, new product drops and information from the world's leading sock brands. Sock Club London also partners with other brands to bring out collaborative product that is exclusively available on the Sock Club London website. The club's motto is 'No Apologies, No Regrets', which stands for its founders' willingness to try new things, push boundaries, make mistakes and learn from them and put themselves out there. Such as writing a rule book all about socks.

If you wish to find out more or become a member, please go to www.sockclublondon.com

ACKNOWLEDGEMENTS

Words: member 001   **Images:** member 002

Sock Club London: Would like to acknowledge that they spent the advance for this book on socks.

Sock Club Londons member 001 and member 002 would like to thank member 003 and member 004, without whose patience and support this book would never have been possible; member 005 for his contribution to and assistance with our product collaborations; member 007 for his guidance, generosity and unwavering support; and all the other members of Sock Club London for their commitment to the cause, for championing men's hosiery and consistently upholding the Rules.

Picture credits: 10 © Victoria and Albert Museum, London; 11 The Print Collector/Corbis; 32 Thomaspajot/Dreamstime.com; 86 Ray Pietro/Getty Images

Commissioning Editor: Joe Cottington
Senior Editor: Alex Stetter
Copy Editor: Marion Paull
Art Director: Juliette Norsworthy
Design: Geoff Fennell

Illustrations: Grace Helmer
Picture Research: Jennifer Veall
Senior Production Manager: Katherine Hockley